FROM THE FILMS OF

Harry Potter

ORIGAMI

VOLUME 2

Copyright © 2021 Warner Bros. Entertainment Inc.
WIZARDING WORLD characters, names and related indicia are © & ™ Warner Bros. Entertainment Inc.
WB SHIELD: © & ™ WBEI. Publishing Rights © JKR. (s21)

ISBN 978-1-338-74518-4

10 9 8 7 6 5 4 3 2 1   21 22 23 24 25

Printed in the U.S.A. 40 • First printing 2021

Origami designs, instruction text, diagrams and photography by Nick Robinson

Hufflepuff Badger design by Lee Armstrong and Flying Ford Anglia design by Kosho Uchiyama

Illustrations by Patrick Spaziante • Additional writing by Kate Lloyd • Book design and project management by Amazing15

Special thanks to Theresa Hong, The British Origami Society, Ali, Daisy & Nick Jnr, plus cats Pickle & Rhubarb

SCHOLASTIC INC.

CONTENTS

* The more lightning bolts, the more difficult!

INSIDE the MAGIC

ORIGAMI is the Japanese art of folding paper into **ANIMALS, OBJECTS, KNIGHT BUSES, DEMENTORS,** and more! Each magical item you will learn to craft in this book can be broken down into a series of basic folds and shapes. It's helpful to practice the basic folds before combining them into more complicated pieces.

Here's an up-close look at the basic folds and symbols you will master over the course of this book.

TIP: We recommend completing each paper craft in the order they come in the book.

ORIGAMI SYMBOLS

Over the past 50 years, origami instructions (known as "diagrams") have been refined and expanded, but a core set of 15 (or so) special folding symbols are still consistently used, which we will look at over the next few pages. These are universally recognized and give enough information for you to understand diagrams regardless of the language that may be employed. After a while, they will become second nature to you, and you will easily be able to follow them.

FOLD ARROWS

A solid line with an arrowhead at one end shows you the direction of the fold.

If it doesn't matter which direction you fold in (such as a basic diagonal crease), both arrowheads will be solid.

On many occasions, you will need to make a crease, then unfold it, creating the crease for later use. The "fold and unfold" line will have an arrowhead at both ends.

A hollow half-arrow head indicates a mountain fold.

An unfolded crease is shown by a very thin, solid line.

BASIC FOLDS

The two most basic folds in origami are the **VALLEY FOLD** and the **MOUNTAIN FOLD**.

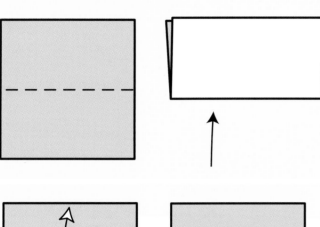

VALLEY FOLD

If you have a sheet of paper on the table in front of you and fold the corner to the opposite corner, you are making a valley fold. Unfold it and you can see the sides rise slightly on either side of the crease, forming a valley in the center. The paper is even slightly V-shaped! The symbol for a valley crease is a series of dashes.

This is what a valley fold and unfold looks like!

PRACTICE MAKES PERFECT!

If you're just starting out, try warming up on some spare paper—the larger the better. Some of the pieces in this book are quite complex, and it will be easier to see your shapes and folds if the paper is bigger.

5

MOUNTAIN FOLD

If you turn an opened valley crease upside down, it becomes what is known as a mountain crease. The two are always formed at the same time. The symbol for a mountain crease is a dash followed by two dots. The fold arrow for a mountain is a solid line with a hollow, half-arrow head.

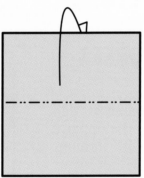

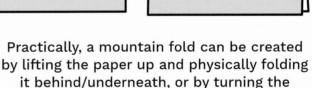

Practically, a mountain fold can be created by lifting the paper up and physically folding it behind/underneath, or by turning the paper over and treating it as a valley fold.

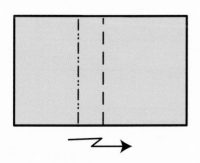

PLEAT

A pleat is simply a combination of a valley and mountain fold. It doesn't matter in which order you make them!

ROTATING AND TURNING THE PAPER

Now that you've practiced the two most basic folds, it's time to move on to paper movement.

TURN OVER ARROW

This small but vital symbol tells you to turn the paper upside down.

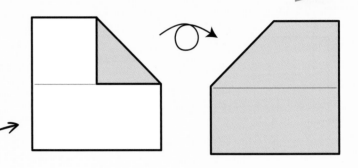

IMPORTANT!
The action is like turning a page in a book so that you see the next page.

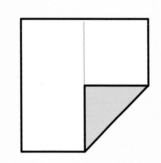

ROTATE 90 DEGREES ARROW

This indicates that the paper has been turned around in the diagram, by 90 degrees or sometimes less. A rotation is usually made so succeeding steps are easier to fold, or it may be so the model is oriented in a familiar way to help you.

ROTATE 180 DEGREES ARROW

Here you are turning the paper around so the lower side is now the upper side. Don't confuse this with turning the paper over! If you see either rotate symbol, simply turn the paper so it looks like the next picture.

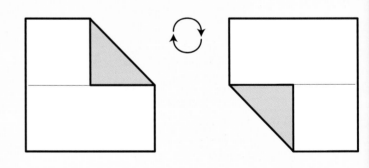

FOLDING TIP

FOLD TO DOTTED LINE

Sometimes it can be hard to see where a corner should be folded to. Checking the next picture always helps, but in this book, a dotted line is shown to help locate some folds.

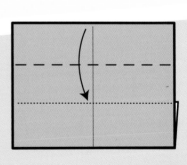

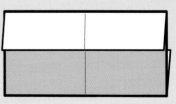

6

ADVANCED FOLDS

Master these and you'll have a shortcut when you work on the more complex pieces in this book.

PULL OUT

When paper has been folded inward, it sometimes needs to be pulled out again. The hollow white arrow is used to indicate pull out, unfold, ease out, and so on. You may need to partially unfold the paper in order to achieve this, but it's normally straightforward.

 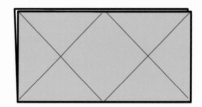

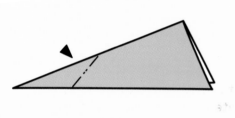

PRESS IN

A solid black triangular shape means apply gentle pressure or push inside. It's used to indicate reverse folds as well as pressing two sides together and a few other situations.

REPEAT ARROW

When a move needs to be repeated, for example, on each corner of a square, the quickest way to indicate this is to use a repeat arrow. Refer to the next picture to see how many times to repeat.

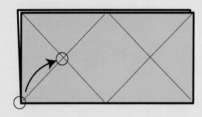

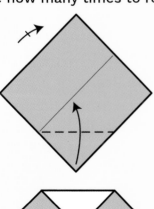

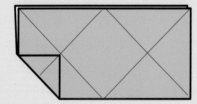

FOLD TO CIRCLES

You'll notice small circles in the diagrams for many of the crafts in this book. They are there to show you exactly where your fold should begin and end.

THE **KNIGHT BUS**

ONE PART

THE KNIGHT BUS is a purple triple-decker bus that picks up stranded members of the wizarding world and transports them to where they want to go. Driven by a British wizard named Ernie Prang at a speed that has his passengers hanging on to anything that's stuck down, this magical vessel comes to Harry's rescue after he causes his aunt Marge to swell up like a balloon and is forced to flee the Dursleys. The Knight Bus can accommodate nine passengers—three on each deck.

DIFFICULTY: ⚡ ⚡ ⚡ ⚡ ⚡

How to Make the KNIGHT BUS

All aboard the Knight Bus! Next stop the Leaky Cauldron. Unlike bus driver Ernie, it's best to take this origami nice and slow.

Start with your paper this way up and then turn the paper over.

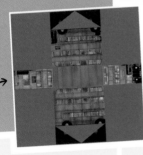

1 White-side up, fold in half, make two pinches, then unfold.

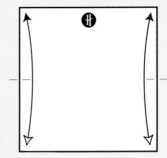

2 Make pinches for the lower quarters, repeat at the top.

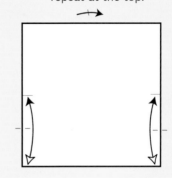

3 Fold the lower edges to the nearest pinches, then unfold. Repeat at the top.

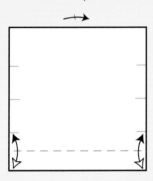

4 Fold the lower corners to the farthest crease, crease, and unfold. Repeat at the top. Turn over.

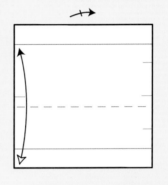

5 Crease where shown, then unfold. Repeat three times.

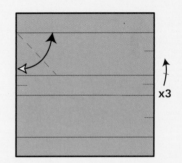

x3

6 Turn the paper over and rotate 90 degrees.

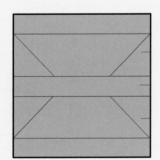

7 Make a horizontal crease through the circled points. Repeat at the top. Rotate 90 degrees.

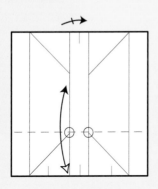

8 Using these creases, begin to make the paper 3-D.

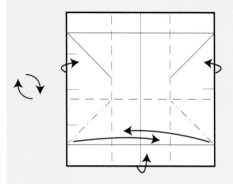

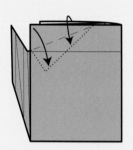

9 The move in progress.

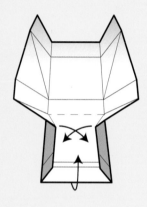

10 This is the result. Fold all the layers down to match the dotted line.

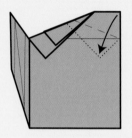

11 Repeat on the right side.

12 Now we focus on the circled area.

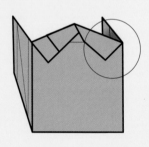

13 Fold the corner to the dotted line.

14 The move is complete. Repeat on the left side.

15 Fold the flap inside, allowing the wheels to slip upward.

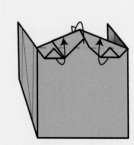

16 Repeat steps 10–14 on the opposite side. Turn the model around.

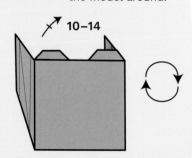

10–14

DONE!

RAVENCLAW RAVEN

ONE PART

The **RAVENCLAW RAVEN** is the emblematic animal of Ravenclaw. One of the four student houses at Hogwarts, Ravenclaw is named after Rowena Ravenclaw, the brilliant medieval witch who helped found Hogwarts, together with Godric Gryffindor, Helga Hufflepuff, and Salazar Slytherin. Ravenclaws are known for being witty, creative, intelligent, and accepting. Filius Flitwick, Luna Lovegood, Cho Chang, and Gilderoy Lockhart are all Ravenclaws.

DIFFICULTY: ⚡ ⚡ ⚡ ⚡ ⚡

How to Make a
RAVENCLAW RAVEN

The end result of this magical make will have you squawking with delight!

Start with your paper this way up and then turn the paper over. →

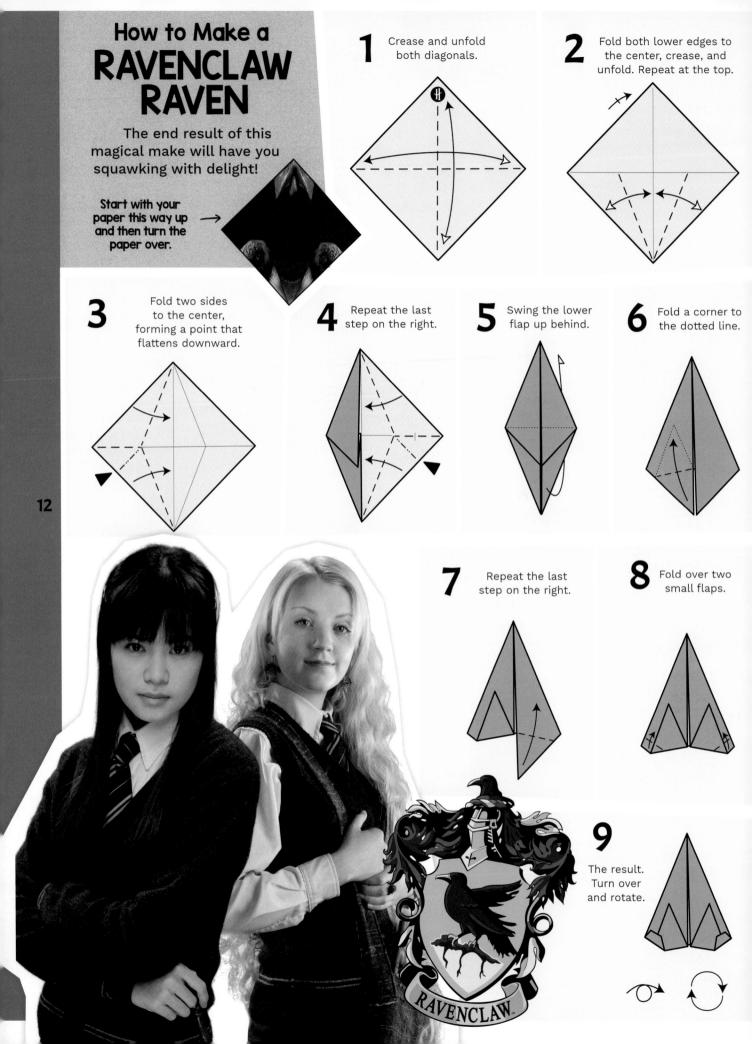

1 Crease and unfold both diagonals.

2 Fold both lower edges to the center, crease, and unfold. Repeat at the top.

3 Fold two sides to the center, forming a point that flattens downward.

4 Repeat the last step on the right.

5 Swing the lower flap up behind.

6 Fold a corner to the dotted line.

7 Repeat the last step on the right.

8 Fold over two small flaps.

9 The result. Turn over and rotate.

10 Fold a flap to the dotted line.

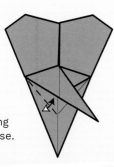

11 Make two pre-creases at a shallow angle.

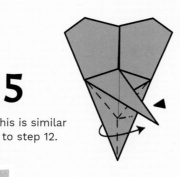

12 Fold the three valley creases, flattening to form the mountain crease.

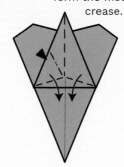

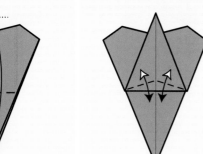

13

(A) Fold edge to edge, creasing where shown.
(B) Swing the beak flap to the right.

14 Add a matching pre-crease.

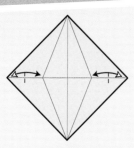

15 This is similar to step 12.

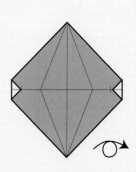

DONE!

13

BONUS!
Follow these bonus instructions if you fancy giving your raven folded eyes.

1 Start at the beginning of step 3 (main). Make two pinch marks. Turn over.

2 Fold to the pinch marks.

3 The result. Follow steps 4–6 of the original sequence.

4 Fold as before to step 6. Fold over two flaps.

5 Fold two corners behind. Rotate 180 degrees then continue with steps 10–15.

6 Focus on the circled area.

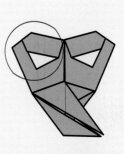

7 Fold over.

8 Lift and squash flat.

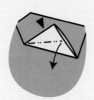

9 Repeat steps 7–8 on the other eye. Lift up the beak.

7–8

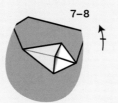

DONE!

GRYFFINDOR LION

ONE PART

The **GRYFFINDOR LION** is the emblematic animal of Gryffindor, one of the four student houses at Hogwarts School of Witchcraft and Wizardry. Gryffindors are known for being courageous, brave, determined, and daring—just like a lion. Gryffindor house is named after Godric Gryffindor, one of the four founders of Hogwarts. Harry Potter, Hermione Granger, Neville Longbottom, Minerva McGonagall, and Ron, Fred, George, and Ginny Weasley are all Gryffindors.

DIFFICULTY: ⚡ ⚡ ⚡ ⚡ ⚡

How to Make a GRYFFINDOR LION

Create your own magnificent Gryffindor lion by following these simple steps. Don't worry, he won't bite!

Start with your paper this way up. →

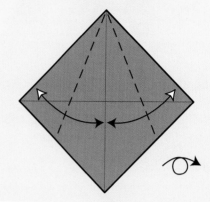

1 Crease and unfold both diagonals.

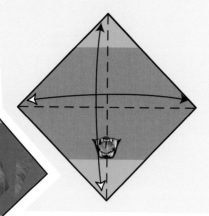

2 Fold the upper edges to the center, crease, and unfold. Turn over.

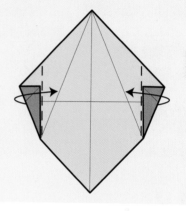

3 Make pre-creases using the circled points as a reference. Turn over.

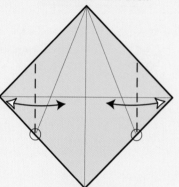

4 Fold in to the vertical creases.

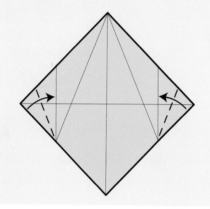

5 Fold over on the vertical creases.

6 Fold the top corner to the dotted (imaginary) line, pinch in the center. Zoom in.

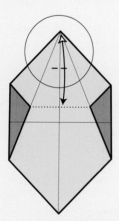

7 Fold the top corner to the pinch, crease, and unfold.

8 Fold the same corner to the recent crease.

9 And fold over again.

10 The result. Turn over.

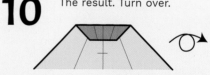

11 Fold in on existing creases.

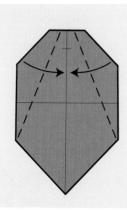

12 Fold down along an edge.

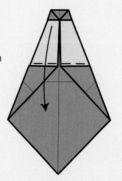

13 Fold the white area upward.

14 Fold the lower corner to the edge, crease, and unfold. Turn over.

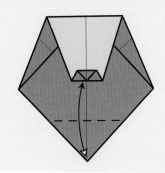

15 Fold so the circled points meet, crease, and unfold. Repeat in the opposite direction.

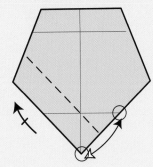

16 Fold using these creases.

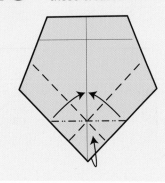

17 Fold the upper flap down and the lower half behind.

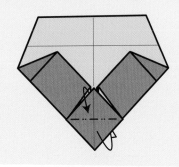

18 Make this crease through all the layers. Turn over.

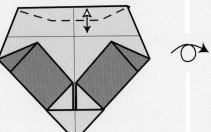

19 Zoom on the circled area.

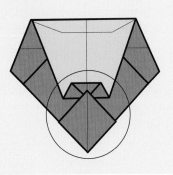

20 Fold the tip down. You can decide how large the mouth is.

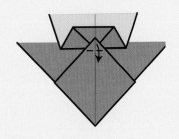

21 Fold over again.

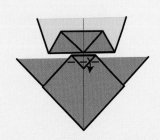

22 Form the model into 3-D, gently shaping the sides of the head.

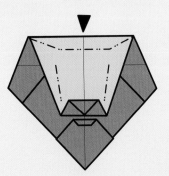

DONE!

HUFFLEPUFF BADGER

The **HUFFLEPUFF BADGER** is the emblematic animal of Hufflepuff, which, like Gryffindor, is one of the four student houses at Hogwarts. Hufflepuff is named after Helga Hufflepuff, an esteemed medieval witch and one of the school's four founders. Hufflepuffs are known for being hardworking, patient, fair, and modest. Triwizard champion Cedric Diggory is a Hufflepuff, as was Newt Scamander, writer of *Fantastic Beasts and Where to Find Them*, many years before him.

DIFFICULTY: ⚡ ⚡ ⚡ ⚡ ⚡

How to Make a HUFFLEPUFF BADGER

Work hard like a Hufflepuff and you'll have perfected this origami badger in no time at all!

Start with your paper this way up.

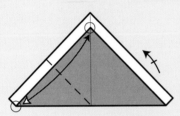

1 White-side up, fold in half, crease, and unfold.

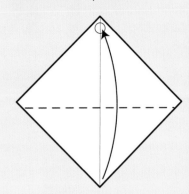

2 Fold the lower corner to just below the top corner.

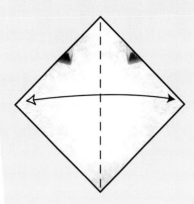

3 Fold so the circled corners meet, crease, and unfold. Repeat on the right.

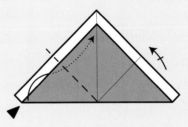

4 Reverse the corner inside. Repeat on the right.

5 The result. Turn over.

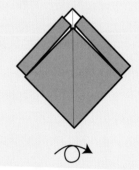

6 Fold an edge to the (imaginary) dotted line. Crease and unfold, then repeat on the right.

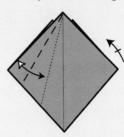

7 Reverse the corner inside. Repeat on the right.

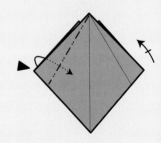

8 The result. Turn over.

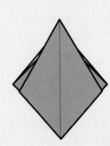

9 Fold a single layer down.

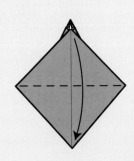

10 Make a short crease where shown.

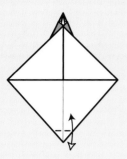

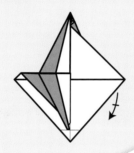

11 Fold a flap down (check the next drawing).

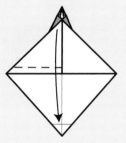

12 Like this. Repeat on the right.

13 Fold the lower corner upward.

14 Ease out and flatten a layer of paper, forming a valley crease along the dotted line.

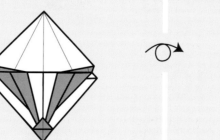

15 Repeat on the right.

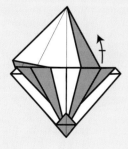

16 The result. Turn over.

17 Fold the top corner down.

18 Fold two layers on an existing crease.

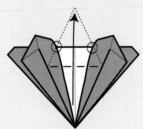

19 Repeat the last step on the right.

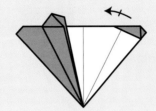

20 Open out the topmost layer on both sides.

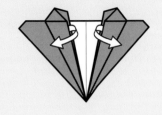

21 Fold up the central flap so edges pass through the circled points. Fold the side flaps at the dotted line.

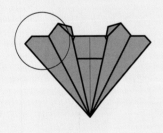

22 Fold the flap behind into a pocket.

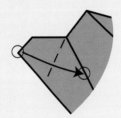

23 Refold the sides inward.

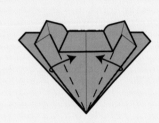

24 Now focus on the circled area.

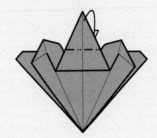

25 Fold so the circled points meet.

26 Tuck the flap under a layer.

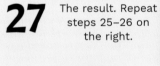

27 The result. Repeat steps 25–26 on the right.

25–26

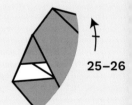

28 Now focus on the circled area.

29 Fold the corner up to match a layer underneath.

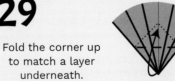

30 Complete. Turn over.

DONE!

SLYTHERIN SNAKE

The **SLYTHERIN SNAKE** is the emblematic animal of Slytherin, the most troublesome of the four Hogwarts student houses (well, if you're a Gryffindor anyway). It was named after the medieval pure-blood wizard and one of the founders of Hogwarts, Salazar Slytherin, before he fled the school in disgrace. Slytherins are known for being resourceful, determined, proud, and cunning. Harry's school rival Draco Malfoy is a Slytherin, while Professor Severus Snape (another of Harry's enemies) is head of Slytherin house.

DIFFICULTY: ⚡ ⚡ ⚡ ⚡ ⚡

How to Make a SLYTHERIN SNAKE

This origami snake is s-s-s-simple when you get going. Just "beware" of the slightly tricky fangs.

← Start with your paper this way up.

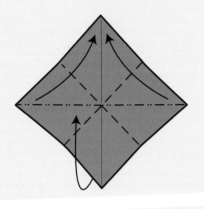

1 Crease and unfold both diagonals. Turn over.

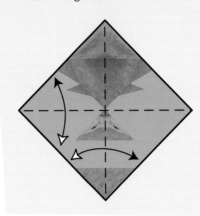

2 Fold the side to the opposite side, crease, and unfold, in both directions.

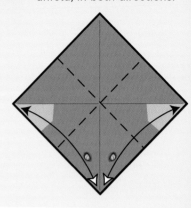

3 Fold the lower corner upward using these creases.

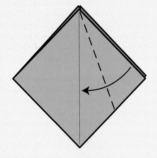

4 Fold down a single corner.

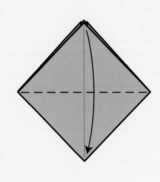

5 Fold a layer from left to right.

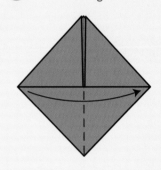

6 Fold an edge to the vertical center.

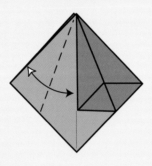

7 Fold the opposite edge to the center, crease, and unfold.

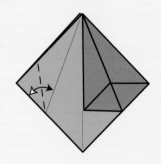

8 Fold the edge to the crease, then unfold.

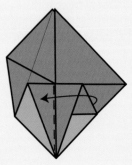

9 Fold a colored edge inside (check the next drawing).

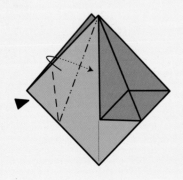

10 Fold the narrow point down.

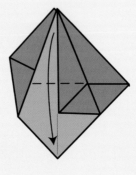

11 Swing a flap from right to left.

12 Swing a flap from right to left.

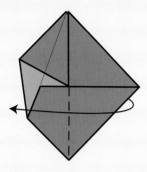

13 Fold the upper left edge to the center.

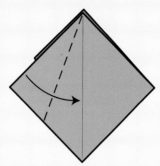

14 Crease and unfold on the right.

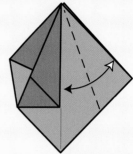

15 Again, crease and unfold on the right.

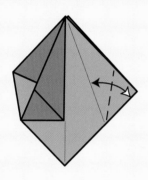

16 Fold in as in step 9.

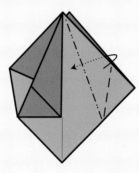

17 Fold the narrow flap down.

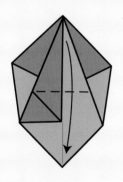

18 Fold a flap to the right so the layers are the same on both sides.

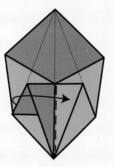

19 Crease and unfold.

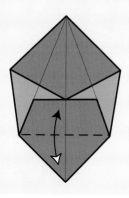

20 Fold the lower left edge over about one-third of the way.

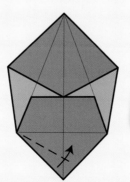

SLYTHERIN.

21 Fold the matching flap over on the right.

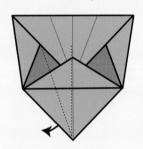

22 Fold down between the wide corners.

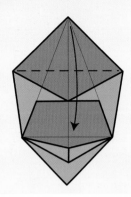
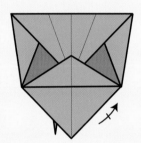

23 Fold up on an existing crease.

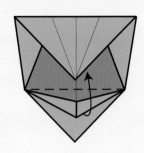
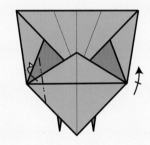

24 Ease out one of the fangs and flatten it in place.

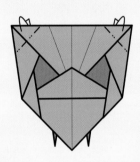

25 Repeat the last step on the right.

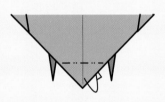

26 Fold some layers behind to shape the head. Repeat on the right.

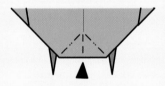

27 Fold the top corners behind to further shape the head.

28 Fold a flap behind.

29 Make these creases, then open the fold to halfway.

30 Like this.

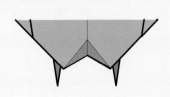

31 That's all the folding done.

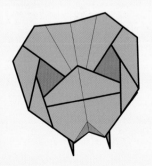

TIP: For bonus decoration, cut out a forked tongue and tape it to the back of the snake's mouth.

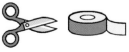

DONE!

24

HARRY'S SCAR

HARRY'S SCAR is the result of a fateful encounter with the Dark wizard Lord Voldemort when Harry is just a baby. Shaped like a lightning bolt, this distinctive mark connects the Boy Who Lived and You-Know-Who. It can even cause Harry pain when the Dark Lord is near. Although troublesome to Harry, his friends all think his lightning bolt scar is really cool.

DIFFICULTY: ⚡ ⚡ ⚡ ⚡ ⚡

How to Make HARRY'S SCAR

Re-create the Boy Who Lived's iconic lightning bolt mark with this simple but effective craft. You'll definitely be "struck" by how much fun it is.

1 Crease and unfold a diagonal.

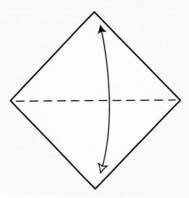

2 Fold the lower left edge to the center.

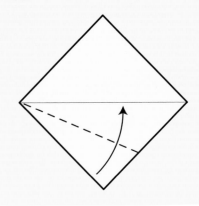

3 Fold the upper right edge to the center.

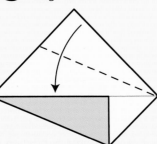

4 Fold the white edges to the center.

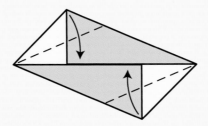

5 Fold the upper and lower corners to the (imaginary) center.

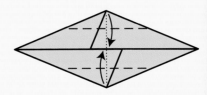

6 Fold the left corner to match the dotted line, creasing where shown, then unfold.

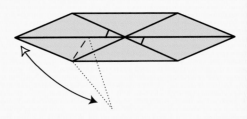

7 Repeat the last step on the upper half. Turn over.

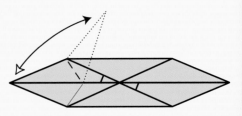

8 Fold so the circled points meet, crease, and unfold. Turn over.

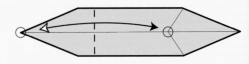

26

9

Fold the upper and lower edges to the vertical crease, making 45-degree creases.

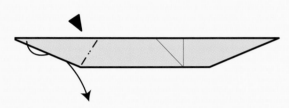

10

Fold in half downward.

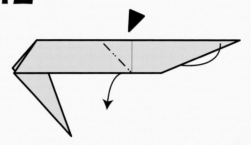

11

Reverse the left corner down between the layers.

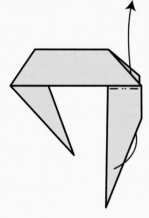

12

Make a similar move on the right.

13

Reverse the flap upward on an existing crease.

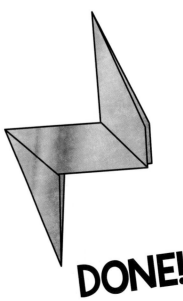

14

Fold so the short left edge lines up with the inside edge. Repeat behind.

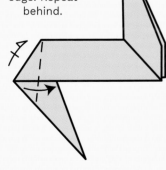

15

Fold over on both sides.

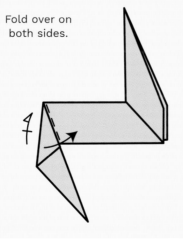

DONE!

HORCRUX RING

Marvolo Gaunt's **HORCRUX RING** is one of Lord Voldemort's seven Horcruxes; it is also his maternal family's ancestral ring. In the wizarding world, Horcruxes are objects in which Dark wizards and witches hide part of their soul in order to live forever. It is difficult, Dark magic that is restricted knowledge at Hogwarts. Unbeknown to Voldemort, the black stone inset in Marvolo's ring is actually the Resurrection Stone, one of the three Deathly Hallows.

DIFFICULTY: ⚡⚡⚡⚡⚡

How to Make a HORCRUX RING

Just like Marvolo Gaunt's ring in the films, there's more to this origami than meets the eye. Enjoy!

1 Fold in half, then unfold.

2 Fold the long edges to the center.

3 Fold in half from left to right.

4 Crease and unfold twice.

5 Reverse a corner inside.

6 Repeat with the lower corner.

7 Fold the upper and lower edges to the center.

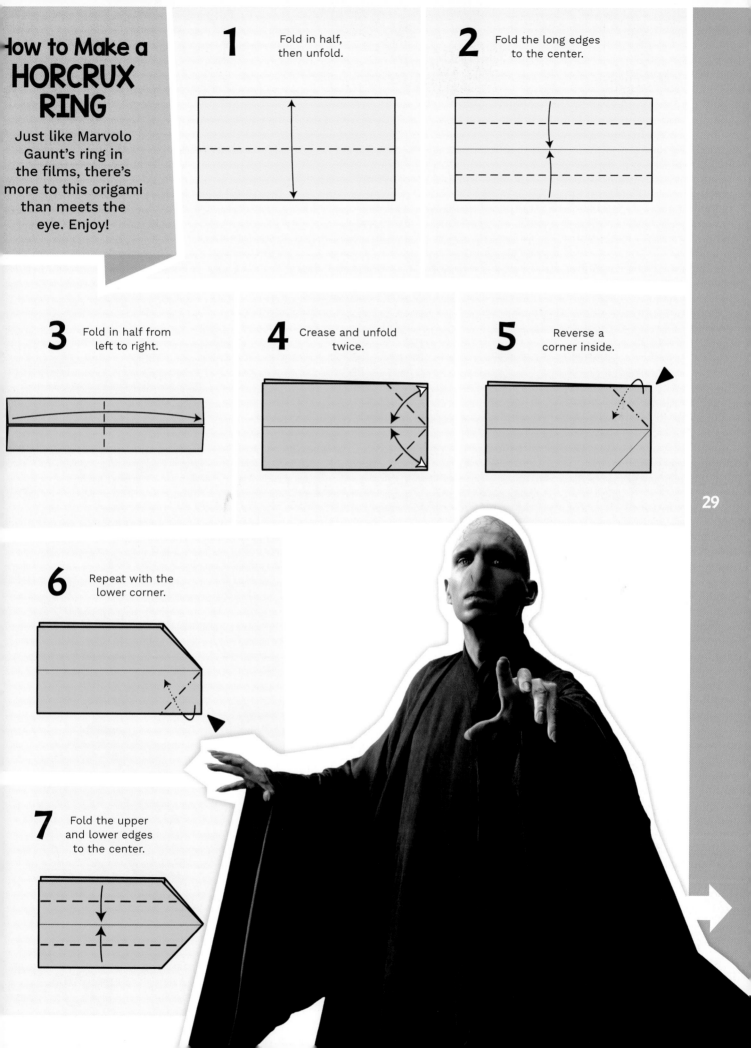

8 This is the result. Turn the paper over.

9 Repeat step 7.

10 Fold the upper flap to the left, crease, and return.

11 We will zoom in to this area.

12 Fold to the dotted line, crease, and unfold.

13 Fold the lower flap behind to the left, allowing the center to open into 3-D.

14 Wrap the ends around, forming a circle.

15 Tuck one end inside the other to form into a ring, like this.

16 Gently press in along these creases.

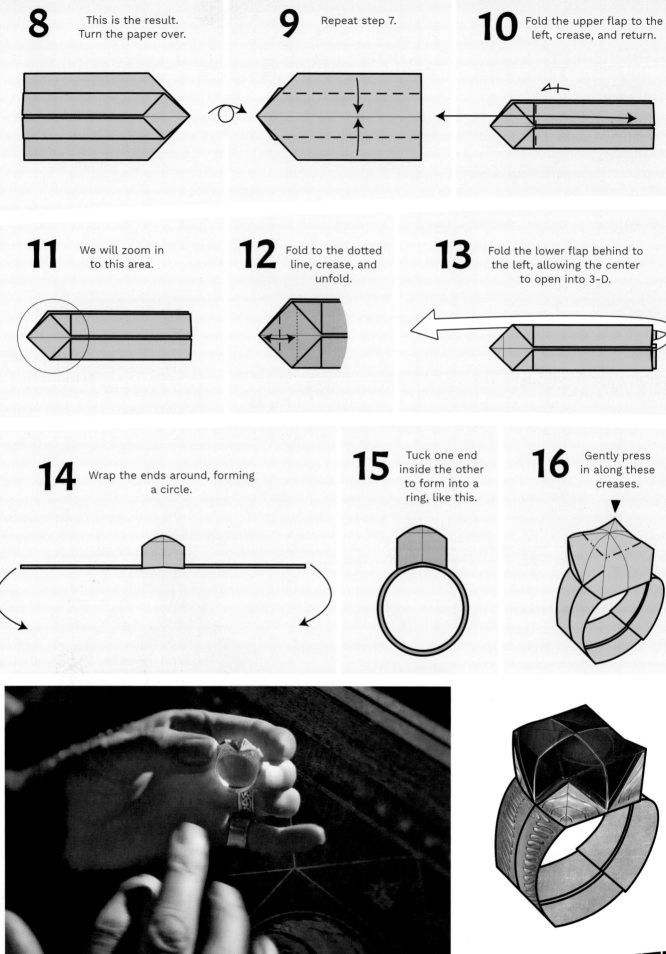

DONE!

MAD-EYE MOODY'S EYE

THREE PARTS

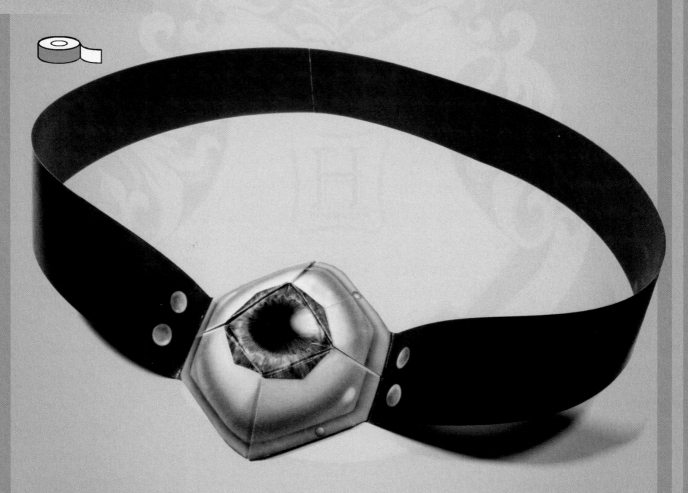

When Alastor "Mad-Eye" Moody becomes the Defense Against the Dark Arts teacher in Harry, Ron, and Hermione's fourth year, the three friends are thrilled (and a little nervous). Moody is one of the most famous Aurors in wizarding history, and his exploits hunting down Dark wizards and witches are legendary. **MAD-EYE MOODY'S EYE**, which he lost in the line of duty, can rotate 360 degrees and enables him to see through anything, including invisibility cloaks and the back of his own head.

DIFFICULTY: ⚡⚡⚡⚡⚡

How to Make
MAD-EYE MOODY'S EYE

You'll need a keen mind and at least one sharp eye for this craft—just like old Mad-Eye himself!

1 Crease in half side to side and unfold in both directions.

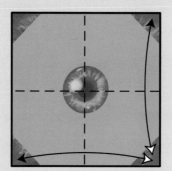

2 Crease and unfold both diagonals.

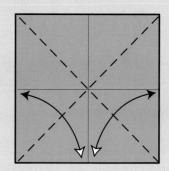

3 Fold all corners to the center.

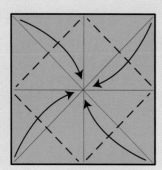

4 The result. Turn over and rotate.

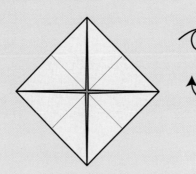

5 Fold the lower edge upward about one-third, creasing between the diagonals. Unfold.

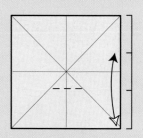

6 Fold the upper edge to the recent crease, making a similar crease.

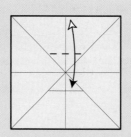

7 Add similar creases on the left and right. Turn over.

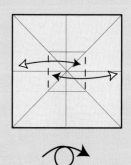

8 Now we focus on the circled area.

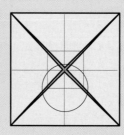

9 Fold an edge to the horizontal crease.

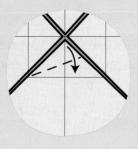

32

10 Make a similar fold on the right side.

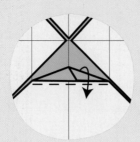

11 Fold the white flap down.

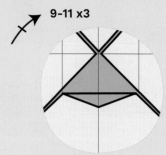

12 Repeat steps 9–11 on the three other sides.

9-11 x3

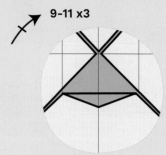

13 The result. Turn over.

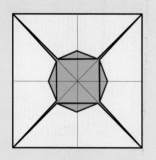

14 Fold two corners to the circled points.

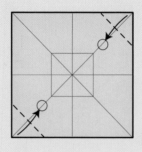

15 Make these two creases to form the paper into 3-D.

3D

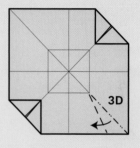

16 Tuck the tip of the flap inside to hold it in place.

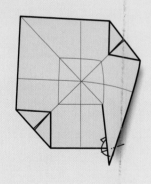

17 Make the same folds on the opposite corner.

15–16

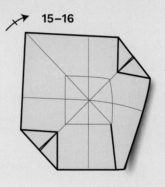

18 The folding is complete. Turn over.

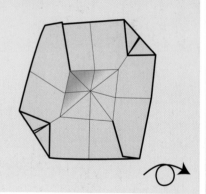

19 The folded eye. Turn over to attach the straps.

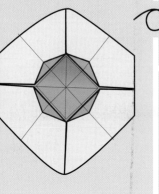

20 Using tape, attach the strap behind these flaps.

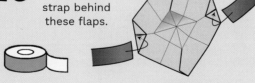

21 Wrap the ends around your head forming a circle. Stick the ends together with tape.

↖ **REMEMBER!**
Be extra careful when putting paper or tape near your eyes!

DONE!

SCABBERS THE RAT

"Pathetic, isn't he?" says Ron Weasley about **SCABBERS THE RAT** in *Harry Potter and the Sorcerer's Stone* (just before he tries and fails to turn Scabbers yellow). But there's more to the Weasleys' long-standing pet than one might think. As Ron, Harry, and Hermione discover to their shock in *Harry Potter and the Prisoner of Azkaban*, Scabbers is actually the Dark wizard Peter Pettigrew in his Animagus form.

DIFFICULTY: ⚡⚡⚡⚡⚡

How to Make SCABBERS

This origami rat is so cute you'll want to make him some friends to play with.

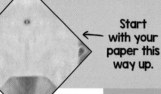

Start with your paper this way up.

1 White-side up, fold in half, crease, and unfold.

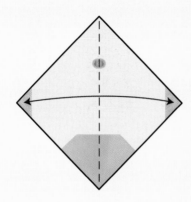

2 Fold both lower edges to the center crease.

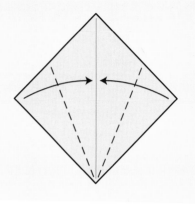

3 Fold the top corner down a little.

4 Fold the corner down as if the corner was there.

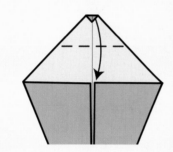

5 Fold so the colored edges meet, crease, and unfold. Repeat on the right. Turn the paper over.

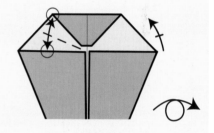

6 Fold the upper section downward.

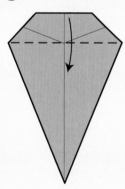

7 Fold along the colored edge, crease, and unfold. Repeat on the right. Turn over.

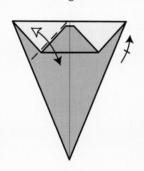

8 Reverse the corner inside. Repeat on the right.

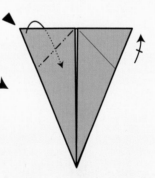

9 Open and flatten two flaps.

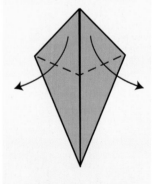

10 Fold the right half behind.

11 Pull out a hidden layer.

12

Rearrange the layers using these creases.

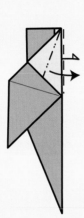

13

Fold the lower flap in half, crease, and unfold.

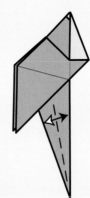

14

Rotate the paper and fold a flap to the right.

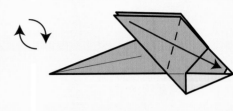

15

Fold the point over just past a hidden edge.

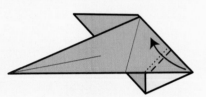

16

Tuck in the flap.

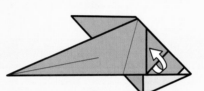

17

Fold a layer inside.

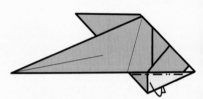

18

Repeat steps 14–17 on the underside.

14–17

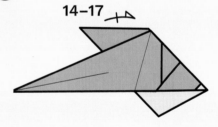

19

Now we focus on the circled area.

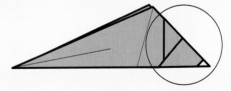

20

Fold the ear in half.

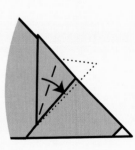

21
Open and squash the pocket (see next drawing).

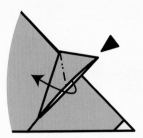

22
Like this. Repeat the last two steps on the underside.

20–21

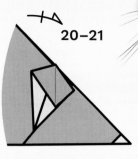

23
Fold half the layers inside between the circled points.

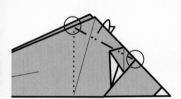

24
Repeat on the underside.

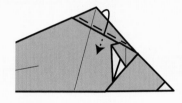

25
Fold the tail to match the dotted line.

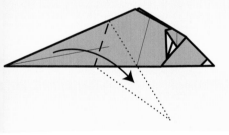

26
Fold to the dotted line and unfold, then open the tail out fully.

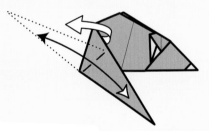

27
Fold the tail in and out again using these creases on both sides.

28
Fold half of the tail inside on both sides.

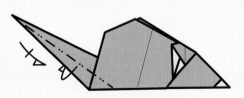

29
Partly open out both ears.

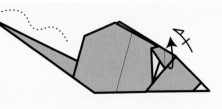

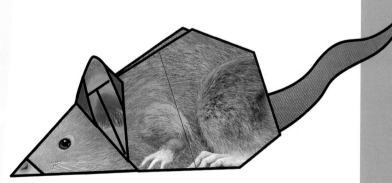

DONE!

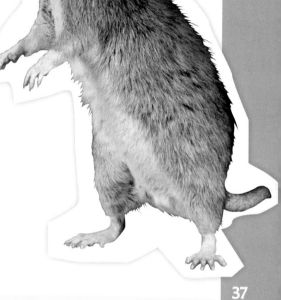

HOGWARTS CREST

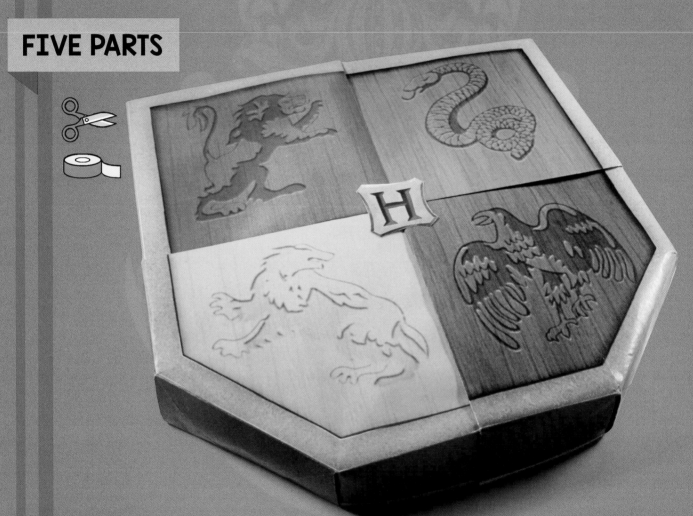

Founded nearly a thousand years ago, Hogwarts School of Witchcraft and Wizardry is arguably the finest school of magic in the wizarding world. Each of the lucky students to pass through its hallowed halls is "sorted" into one of four houses: Gryffindor, Ravenclaw, Hufflepuff, and Slytherin, named after the school's esteemed founders. The emblematic animals of these houses—lion, raven, badger and snake—can be seen on the famous **HOGWARTS CREST**.

DIFFICULTY: ⚡ ⚡ ⚡ ⚡ ⚡

How to Make a
HOGWARTS CREST

Show your school pride with this challenging but rewarding craft.

Start with the Slytherin sheet this way up and turn over. →

1 Turn the sheet over to the white side, then make small pinch marks to mark the halfway points.

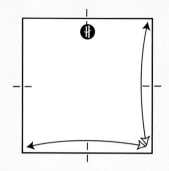

2 Add upper and lower 1/4 creases.

3 Add upper and lower 1/8 creases.

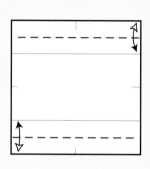

4 Repeat steps 2–3 in the other direction.

2–3

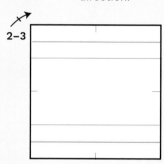

5 Turn over and focus on the circled area.

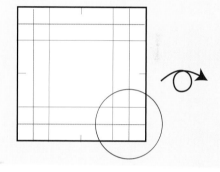

6 Fold this crease only where shown.

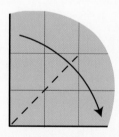

7 Add this crease, then unfold and turn over.

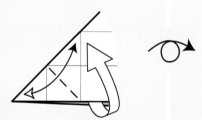

8 Fold over twice on existing creases. Rotate 180 degrees.

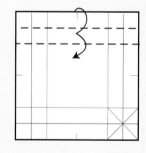

9 Form the paper into 3-D using these creases.

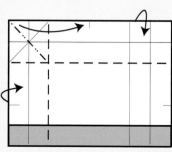

10 Fold the corner behind to trap it.

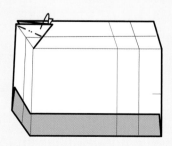

11 Holding the recent folds in place, wrap the edge inside.

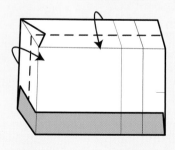

12 Open the model slightly and wrap the right edge underneath.

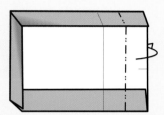

13 The first unit is complete. Make another identical unit.

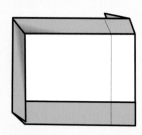

Use the Gryffindor sheet next. Start with it this way up and then turn over.

14 Rotate the second unit to this position. Slightly unfold the upper left corner.

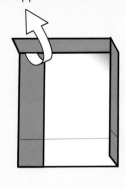

15 Tuck the flap of the green unit into the pocket of the red unit.

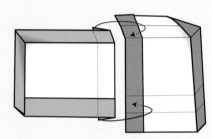

16 Refold the flap inward.

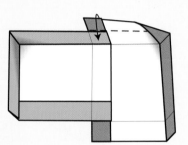

17 The first two units are in place. Now we fold the other two.

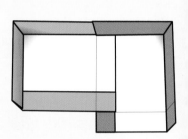

DRACO DORMIENS NUNQUAM TITILLANDUS

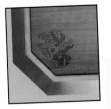

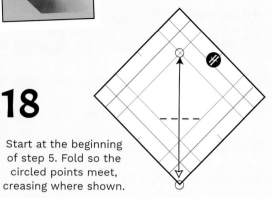

The Ravenclaw sheet is the next to use. Start this way up and turn over. ←

18

Start at the beginning of step 5. Fold so the circled points meet, creasing where shown.

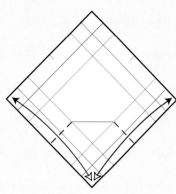

19 Make two more pre-creases where shown.

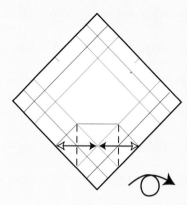

20 Circle the three outer edges (all but the top) to indicate where shown. Turn over.

21 Focus on the circled area.

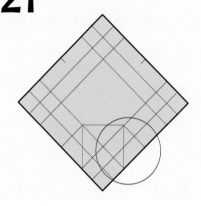

22 Fold so the short creases line up.

23 Make sure the circled creases line up, then unfold.

24 Repeat steps 22–23 on the left. Turn over.

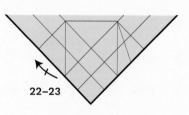

22–23

25 Fold the lower corner upward.

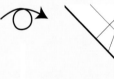
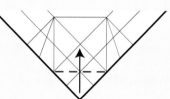

26 Fold upward so the circled points meet.

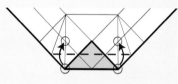

27 Fold the lower edge to the crease, then unfold.

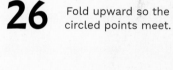

28 Unfold a layer. Rotate the paper.

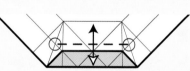
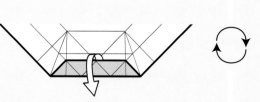

29 Fold an edge over twice.

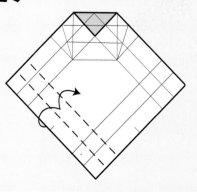

41

30
Form the paper into 3-D using these (existing) creases.

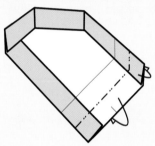

31
Fold over the colored flap.

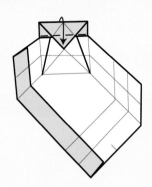

32
Holding the recent folds in place, wrap the edge inside.

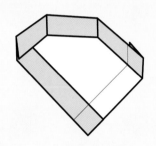

33
Open the model slightly and wrap the white edge underneath.

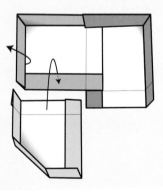

34
The third unit is complete. Make another identical unit.

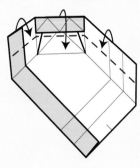

The final sheet to fold is Hufflepuff! Start with it this way up and turn over.

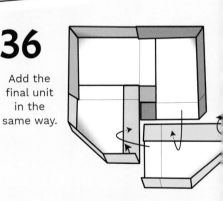

35
Open a flap and join the third unit as in steps 15–16. Recent folds may start to come apart. Be patient and fold carefully!

36
Add the final unit in the same way.

37
Complete. Sharpen all creases and turn over.

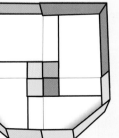

TIP: For bonus decoration, cut out the Hogwarts "H" and stick it to the center of the crest.

DONE!

HATCHING NORBERT

As Harry Potter and his fellow champions discover in *Harry Potter and the Goblet of Fire*, fully grown dragons are not to be messed with (especially Hungarian Horntails). Baby dragons, however, are another matter entirely. While still capable of burning a hut down if left unattended, they're extremely cute, as Harry, Ron, and Hermione find out when they witness a **HATCHING NORBERT** (as Hagrid decides to call the tiny Norwegian Ridgeback) in the first film.

DIFFICULTY: ⚡⚡⚡⚡⚡

How to Make a
HATCHING NORBERT

You'll give a huge fiery roar when you complete this origami and have a baby dragon of your very own!

← **Start with your paper this way up.**

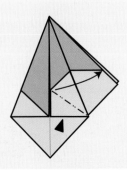

1 Crease and unfold both diagonals. Turn over.

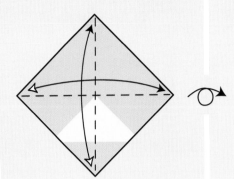

2 Crease in half side to side and unfold in both directions.

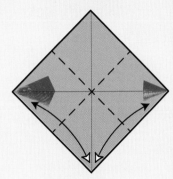

3 Fold the top corner to the center.

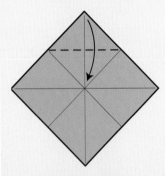

4 Fold the lower corner to the circled point.

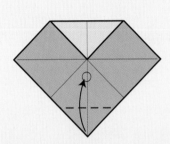

5 Fold the lower edge upward using these creases.

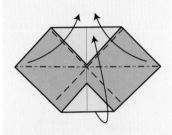

6 Fold a flap from left to right.

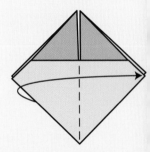

7 Fold the edges to the center.

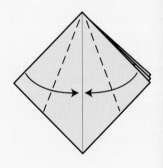

8 Open and squash the layers at the corner.

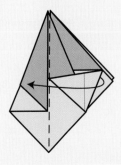

9 Fold a layer from right to left.

10 Fold another flap to the left.

11 Fold the upper edges to the center.

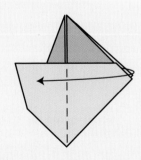

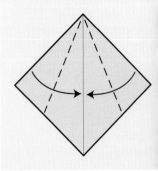

12 Open and squash as in step 8.

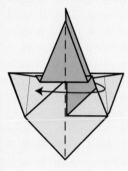

13 Fold the lower flap behind from left to right.

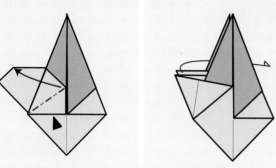

14 Fold the flap down.

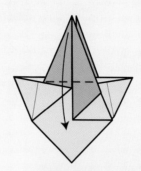

15 Leave a small gap, then fold the flap back up again.

16 Fold a flap from right to left.

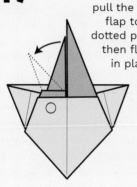

17 Hold at the circled point, pull the narrow flap to the dotted position, then flatten in place.

18 Make a short, firm crease where shown. Turn over.

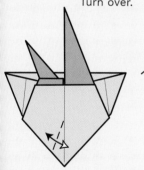

19 Start to make the two creases shown, then flatten the flap to match the dotted line.

20 Fold behind the pointed end of the head to create the dragon's nose.

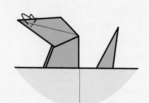

21 Fold two corners behind to shape the egg.

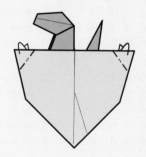

22 Form a pleat using these creases. The egg becomes 3-D.

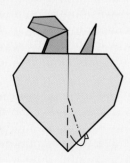

23 Fold this paper behind, flattening it on the underside.

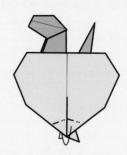

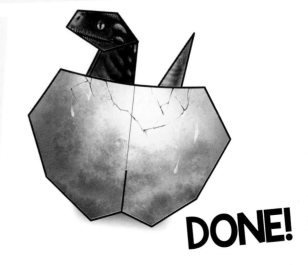

DONE!

FLYING FORD ANGLIA

Arthur Weasley's **FLYING FORD ANGLIA** is a magically modified Muggle car that comes to Harry and Ron's rescue when they are unable to access platform nine and three-quarters at King's Cross station in *Harry Potter and the Chamber of Secrets*. Having missed the Hogwarts Express, the young friends fly the Ford Anglia to Hogwarts, eventually crash-landing in the school's Whomping Willow tree—something they quickly come to regret when the tree fights back. Ouch!

DIFFICULTY: ⚡ ⚡ ⚡ ⚡ ⚡

How to Make a FLYING FORD ANGLIA

Harry and Ron enjoy the ride of their life in Mr. Weasley's Ford Anglia, and you'll have lots of fun with this craft, too.

Start with your paper this way up and then turn the paper over. →

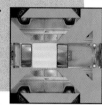

1 White-side up, fold in half, crease, and unfold. Repeat in the other direction.

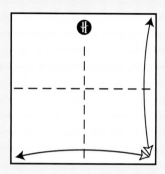

2 Fold the upper and lower edges to the center, crease, and unfold.

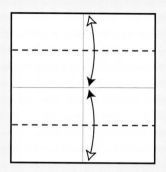

3 Fold the upper and lower edges to the nearest creases, then unfold.

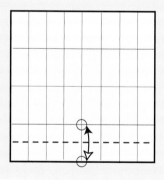

4 Fold so the circled points on each side meet, crease, and unfold. Rotate the paper 90 degrees.

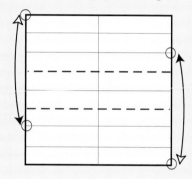

5 Fold so the circled points on each side meet, adding 1/4 creases.

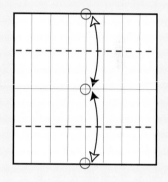

6 Fold the lowest edge to the 1/4 crease, then unfold.

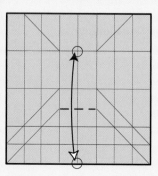

7 Fold so the circled points meet, creasing where shown, then unfold. Repeat in the other direction. Turn over.

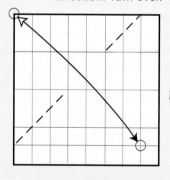

8 Fold so the circled points meet, creasing where shown, then unfold. Repeat in the other direction.

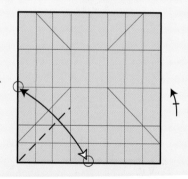

9 Add this small crease.

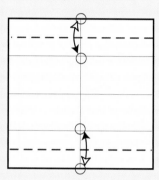

10 Fold so the circled points meet, making a short crease where shown, then unfold. Repeat in the other direction. Turn over.

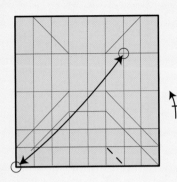

11 Fold the upper edge down to the center.

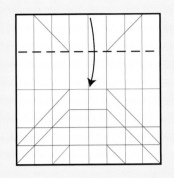

12 Lift up the mountain fold, then fold it to the crease, making a new crease in the center. The left side of the paper will curl around and not lie flat.

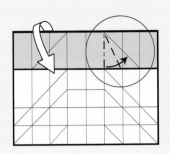

13 The paper should look like this. Add a small valley crease through the colored layer, then unfold to step 12.

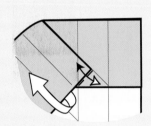

14 Repeat the last two steps on the other side.

12–13

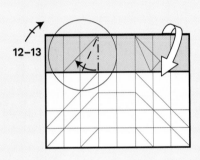

15 Lift up the colored flap and turn the paper over.

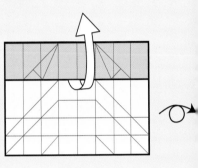

16 Fold using these creases. The paper becomes 3-D.

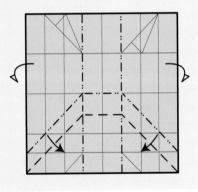

17 Fold the side flaps inward, bringing the front edge down.

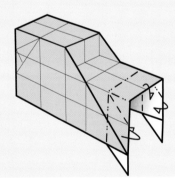

18 Fold the white flaps underneath a layer, then crease firmly.

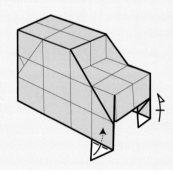

19 Fold on these creases to lower the trunk of the car.

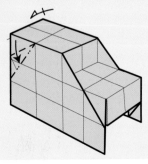

20 Like this. We will focus on the circled area.

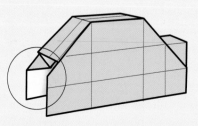

21 Fold the short white edge starting at the circled point, crease, and unfold.

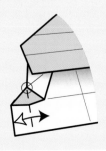

22 Fold the white edge in, lifting up and squashing the colored triangle.

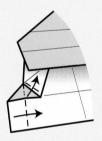

23 The move is complete. Repeat on the other side.

24 Fold the lower corners to meet the dotted lies. Crease firmly.

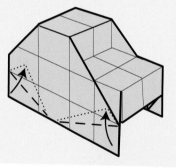

25 Fold the lower flap inside, allowing the wheels to flip down.

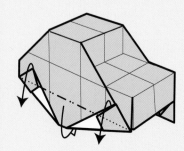

26 Fold the tips of the wheels behind. Repeat steps 24–26 on the other side.

24–26

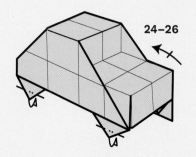

DONE!

DEMENTOR

There are lots of scary creatures in the wizarding world, but among the scariest are Azkaban's Dementors. A **DEMENTOR** is a wraithlike being that feeds on human despair. Harry first meets one on the Hogwarts Express in *Harry Potter and the Prisoner of Azkaban*, and it's only the quick thinking of new professor Remus Lupin that prevents Harry from falling victim to the terrifying Dementor's Kiss. A Dementor can (thankfully) be warded off with the powerful Patronus Charm.

DIFFICULTY: ⚡⚡⚡⚡⚡

How to Make a DEMENTOR

One of the more advanced makes in this book, you'll need to muster all your willpower (just like Harry when he faced a real Dementor) to complete this complex but very cool origami.

Start with your paper this way up. →

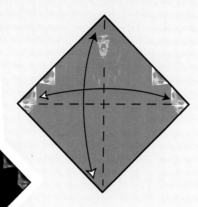

1 Crease and unfold both diagonals.

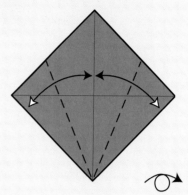

2 Fold the lower edges to the center, crease, and unfold. Turn over.

3 Make pre-creases using the circled point as a reference. Turn over.

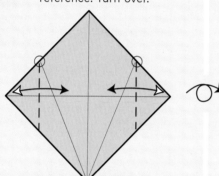

4 Fold in using these creases.

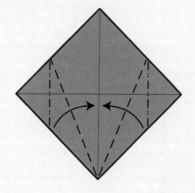

5 Crease the white area in half.

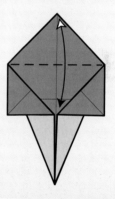

6 Make another pre-crease between the circled points. Turn over.

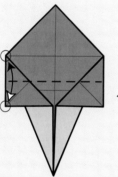

7 Mountain fold the existing crease to the lower corners, forming a new valley. Ignore the existing crease.

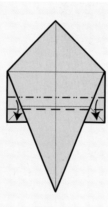

8 Make a similar pleat, again ignoring the existing crease.

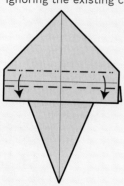

9 Now we focus on the circled area.

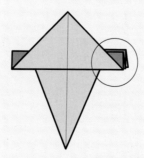

10 Fold a white flap over the edge, crease, and unfold.

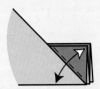

11 Reverse the corner inside.

12 Repeat steps 10–11 on back layer. Then repeat steps 10–12 on the left side.

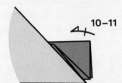

10–11

13 Fold the lower corner to the dotted line.

14 Fold each side of the triangle to the lower edge, pre-creasing where shown.

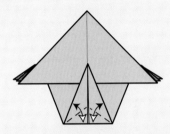

15 Fold the right half behind, forming a point with the valley creases.

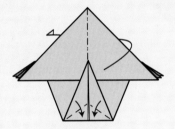

16 Hold the circled area, then pull the point down, flattening into the new position.

17 Open out the upper layer.

18 Form a pleat. The paper will curl around.

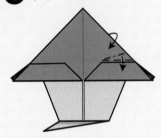

19 Tuck the small flap behind a layer.

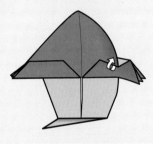

20 Repeat steps 18–19 on the left side.

18–19

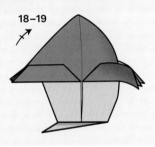

21 Form a small pleat at the top.

22 Fold the pleat inside (you decide how much).

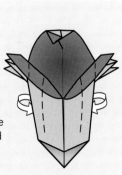

23 Curve and shape the model; these are not hard creases.

DONE!

HOUSE-ELF

ONE PART

HOUSE-ELVES are small, magical creatures with long noses and even longer ears. They are very loyal and obedient and can often be found working as servants for old wizarding families. The Malfoys, for example, have a house-elf named Dobby, who becomes good friends with Harry. Although they don't have wands, house-elves are very powerful. They can only be freed if they are presented with an item of clothing by their master, such as a sock.

DIFFICULTY: ⚡⚡⚡⚡⚡

How to Make a
HOUSE-ELF

Don't do a Dobby and be too hard on yourself if you don't master this origami on your first go. It's a little tricky but you'll get there!

Start with your paper this way up.

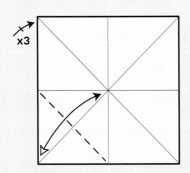

1 Fold in half, crease, and unfold in both directions. Turn over.

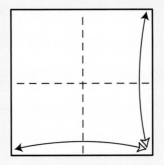

2 Crease and unfold both diagonals.

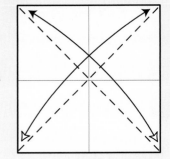

3 Fold a corner to the center, crease, and unfold. Repeat three times.

x3

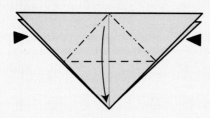

4 Fold using these creases.

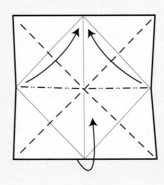

5 Fold the lower corner to the center of the upper edge, crease, and unfold.

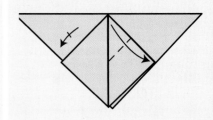

6 Fold the center of the upper edge downward, flattening the points on either side.

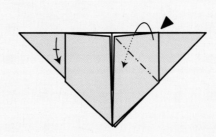

7 Reverse the corner inside. Repeat on the left.

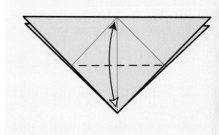

8 Fold an upper corner to the right corner. Repeat on the left.

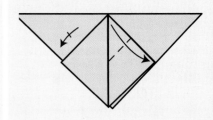

9 Fold a corner to the center, crease, and unfold.

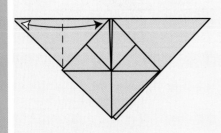

10 Make two pre-creases, dividing the angles in half.

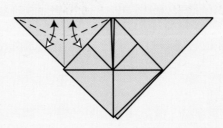

11 Fold the corner to the right, reversing the center of the flap as you do so.

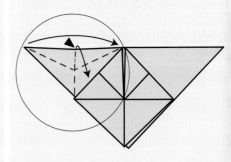

12 Open and asymmetrically flatten the flap—see the next move.

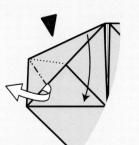

13 Fold part of the flap behind.

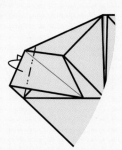

14 Open the flap out, encouraging it to be curved and 3-D.

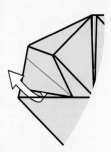

15 The ear is complete. Repeat steps 9–14 on the right side.

9–14

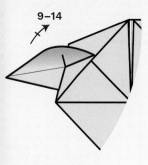

16 Fold a flap upward.

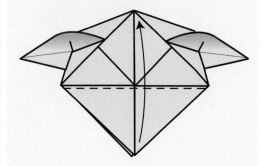

17 Add two pre-creases.

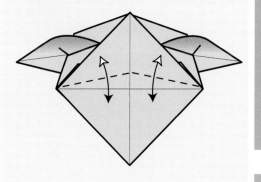

18
Fold the lower corner to the circled point.

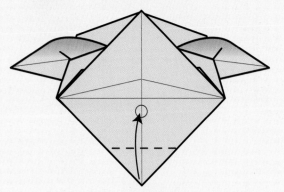

19
Leave a small gap, then fold the flap down again.

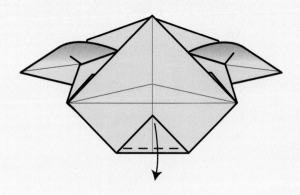

20
Add a curved crease to shape the mouth.

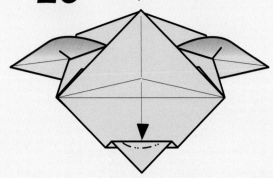

21
Fold three creases to form a pointed nose.

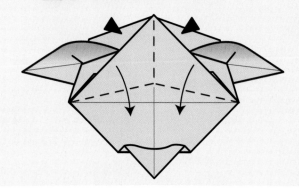

22
Fold flaps behind by the eyes. Shape the nose however you wish!

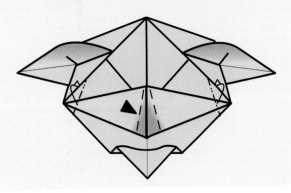

23
Form the head into 3-D using these creases. Turn over.

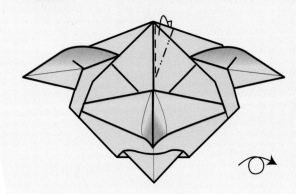

24
Fold a flap behind to "lock" the head into position. Gently curve the sides of the head. Turn over.

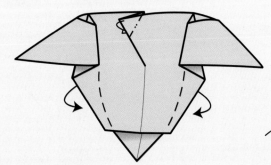

DONE

HAGRID'S HUT

HAGRID'S HUT is a small wooden cabin situated on the edge of the Forbidden Forest, next to the school pumpkin patch. It's home to the half-giant Rubeus Hagrid. Hagrid lives in the hut with his dog, Fang, and various other (usually dangerous) magical creatures. Harry, Ron, and Hermione often visit the hut, where the kindly gamekeeper is always waiting with one of his infamous rock cakes. (It's best to politely decline if you want to keep your teeth!)

DIFFICULTY: ⚡ ⚡ ⚡ ⚡ ⚡

How to Make HAGRID'S HUT

Just like Harry when he visits Hagrid in the films, this craft might initally make you a little nervous (Hagrid's hut is always full of surprises, after all!), but you'll actually have a great time completing it.

Start with your paper this way up and then turn the paper over. →

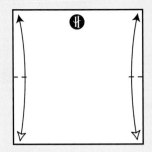

1 White-side up, fold in half, make two pinch marks, and unfold.

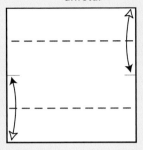

2 Fold the upper and lower edges to the center, crease, and unfold.

3 Mark the center of the lower edge with a pinch.

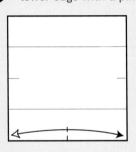

4 Pinch the 1/4 mark.

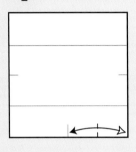

5 Pinch the 1/8 mark.

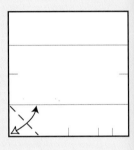

6 Fold the lowest left corner to the crease, then unfold.

7 (Enlarged view!) Fold the lower edge to the recent crease, then unfold.

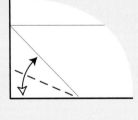

8 Fold the upper and lower edges to the center.

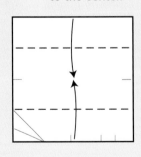

9 Fold the left edge to the farthest pinch mark, crease firmly, and unfold.

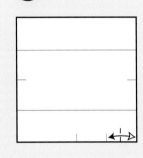

10 Fold the inner corner to the outer edge.

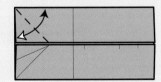

11 Make a pre-crease as in step 7.

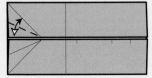

12 Make a crease between the circled points. Check carefully before creasing.

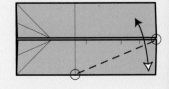

13 Fold the short edge to the outer edge, crease, unfold, then unfold the larger flap.

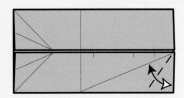

14 Fold the corner down as in step 12.

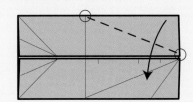

15 Fold the short edge to the outer edge, crease, unfold, then unfold the larger flap.

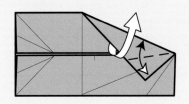

16 Reverse the lower right corner inside.

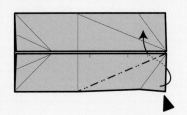

17 Fold the left edge to the crease intersections, then unfold. Rotate the paper.

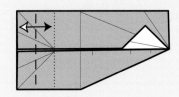

18 This is the completed "unit;" make another four.

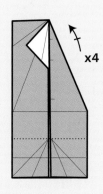

x4

19 Arrange two units like this. The corner of one slides into a pocket inside the white corner of the other.

20 Make sure the two units are tightly interlocked, then fold a flap inside to hold them together.

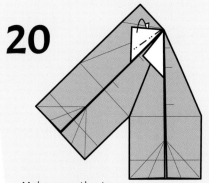

21 Repeat with the three other units.

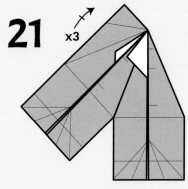

x3

22 Repeat steps 19 and 20 to connect the last unit to the first one. The paper will become (and stay) 3-D from here on.

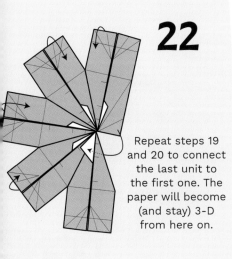

23 Open out a single layer, folding it on top of a layer of the next unit.

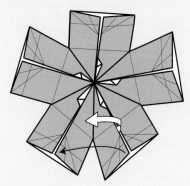

24 Using existing creases, fold a double layer behind.

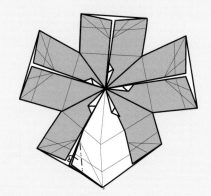

25 Fold over a second time, to secure the paper in place.

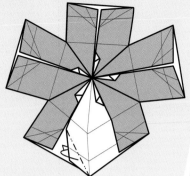

26 Open up another layer and repeat steps 23–25 on each of the units.

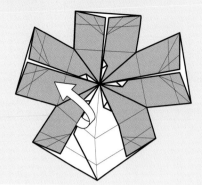

27 Carefully fold the upper edge inside the model.

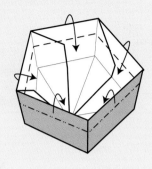

28 Crease firmly when all complete. Lay each face on the table and flatten everything! Turn over.

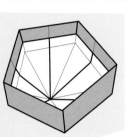

29 Repeat the process with parts 6–10 to make the second, smaller hut.

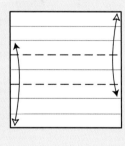

Use part II to build the chimney.

30 Fold in half, crease and unfold.

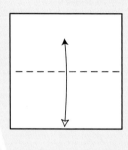

31 Add 1/4 creases.

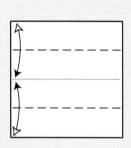

32 Add outside 1/8 creases.

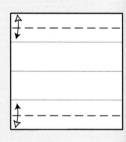

33 Add 3/8 creases.

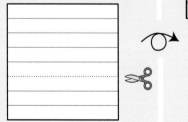

34 Cut along the dotted line. Turn the paper over.

35 Add these small creases and turn the paper over.

36 Fold two sides in. The crease on the right passes through the circled points. On the left, it's not so important!

37 Rotate the paper. Fold the sides in at 90 degrees, lifting a flap at the top.

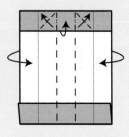

38 Fold in two flaps, sliding one into the other.

39 Complete.

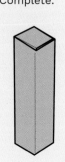

Combine the three models to complete the hut.

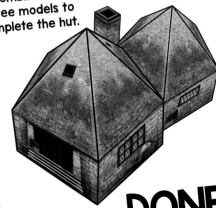

DONE

60

DIFFICULTY: ⚡ ⚡ ⚡ ⚡

THE KNIGHT BUS

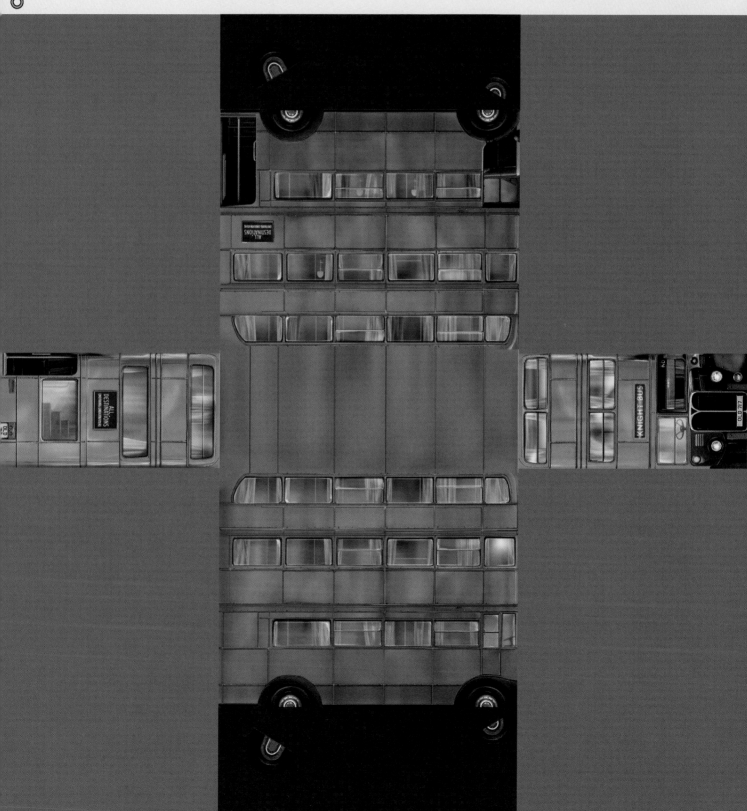

RAVENCLAW RAVEN

GRYFFINDOR
LION

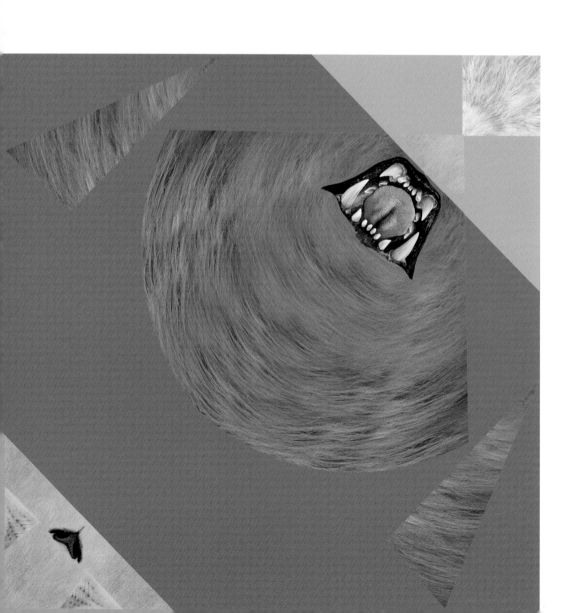

HUFFLEPUFF BADGER

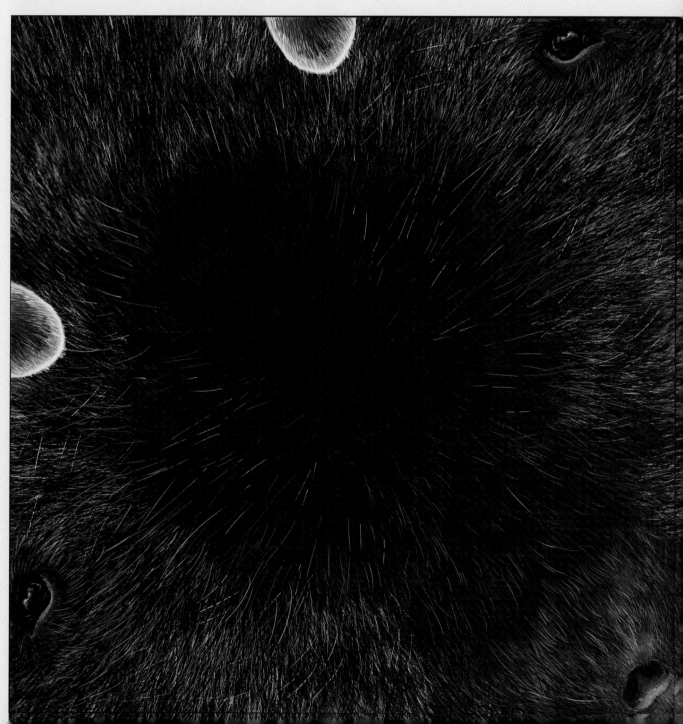

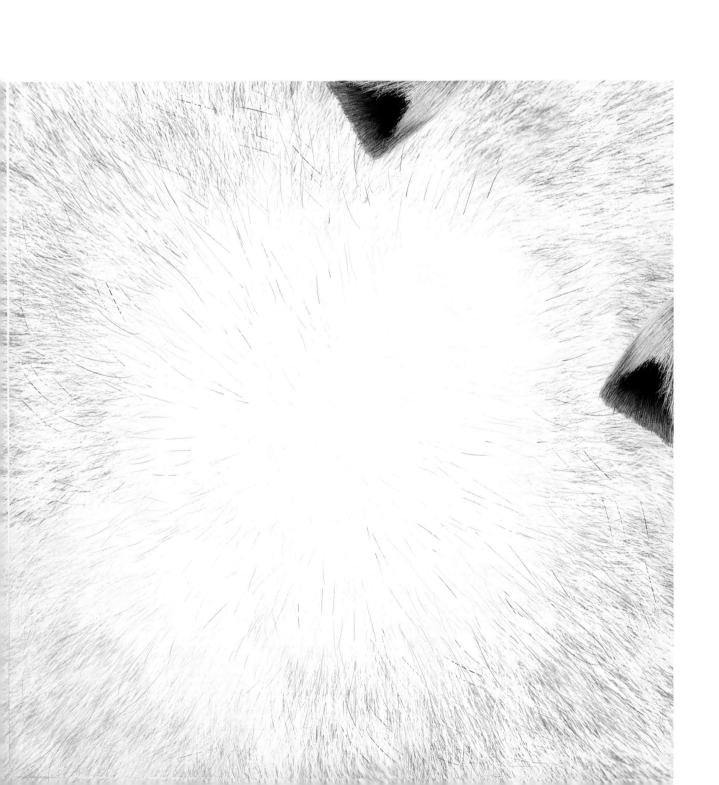

SLYTHERIN SNAKE

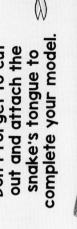

Don't forget to cut out and attach the snake's tongue to complete your model.

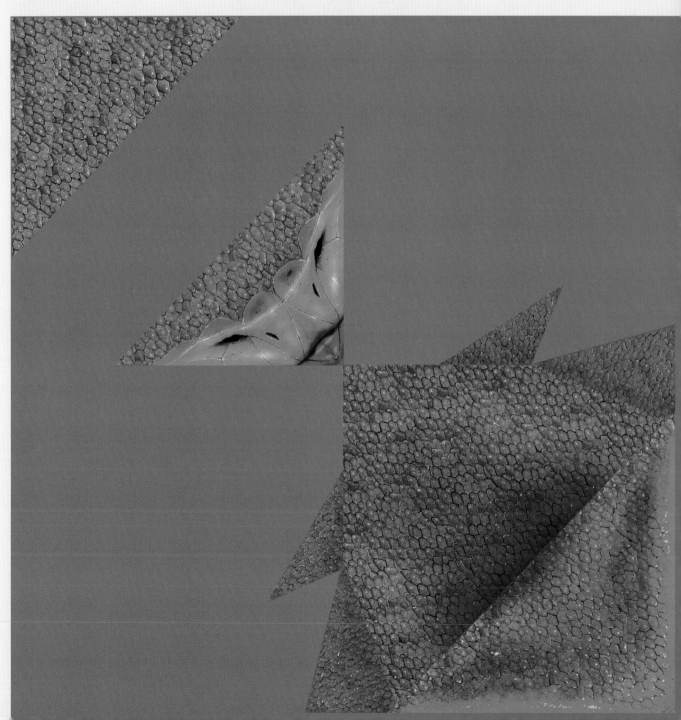

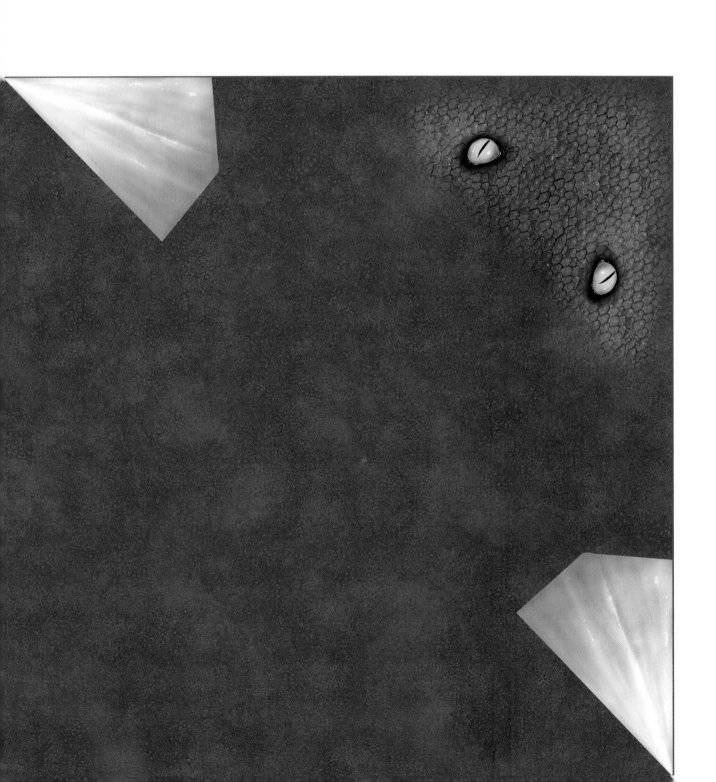

HARRY'S SCAR

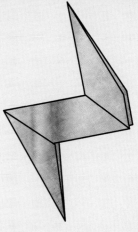

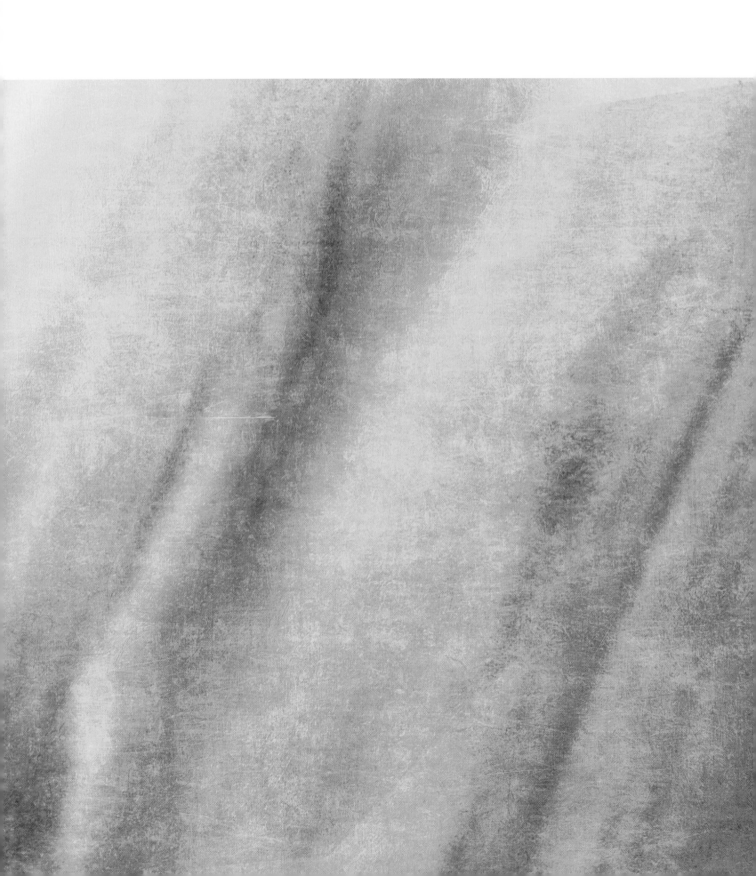

HORCRUX RING

✂ →

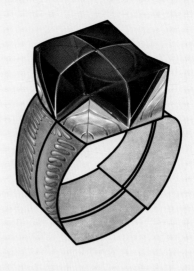

Once you've mastered the larger ring, try folding the smaller one to fit on your finger. ✂ →

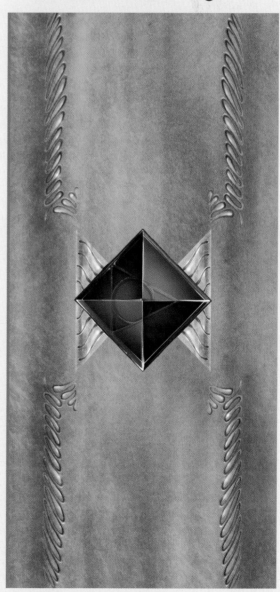

SCABBERS THE RAT

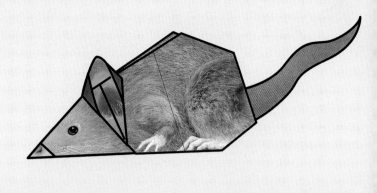

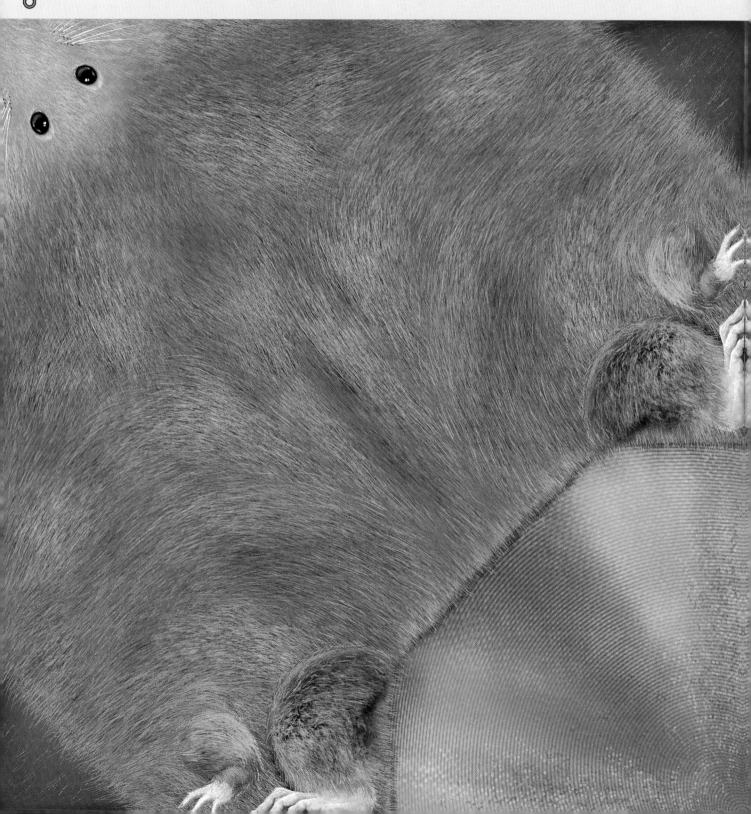

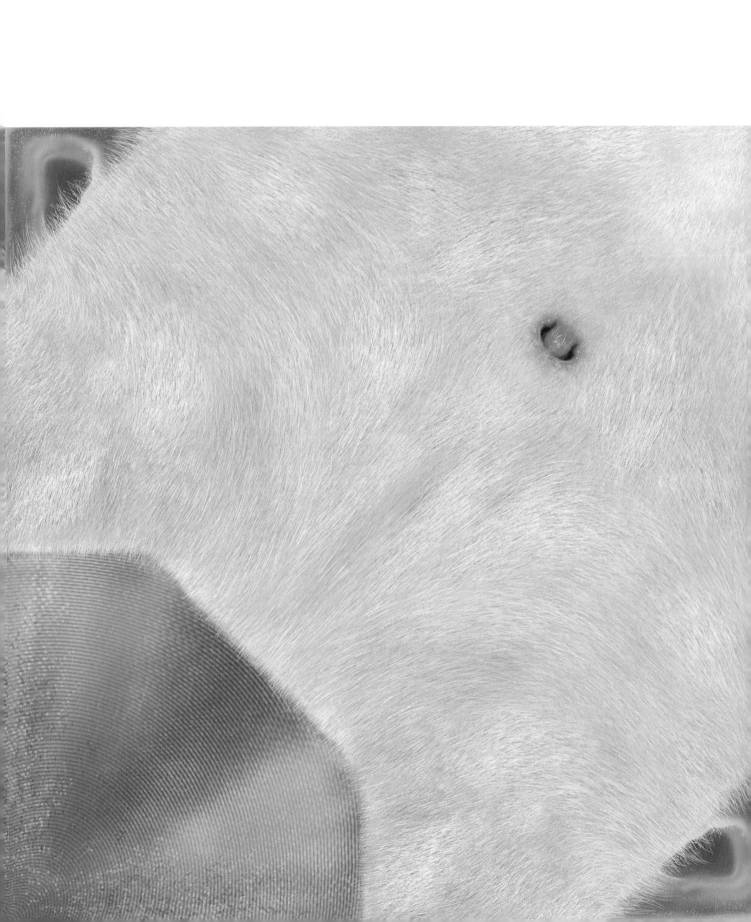

HOGWARTS CREST
I. TOP RIGHT

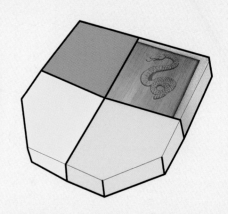

HOGWARTS CREST
II. TOP LEFT

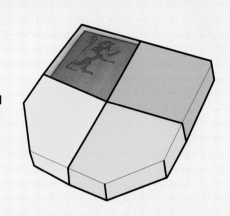

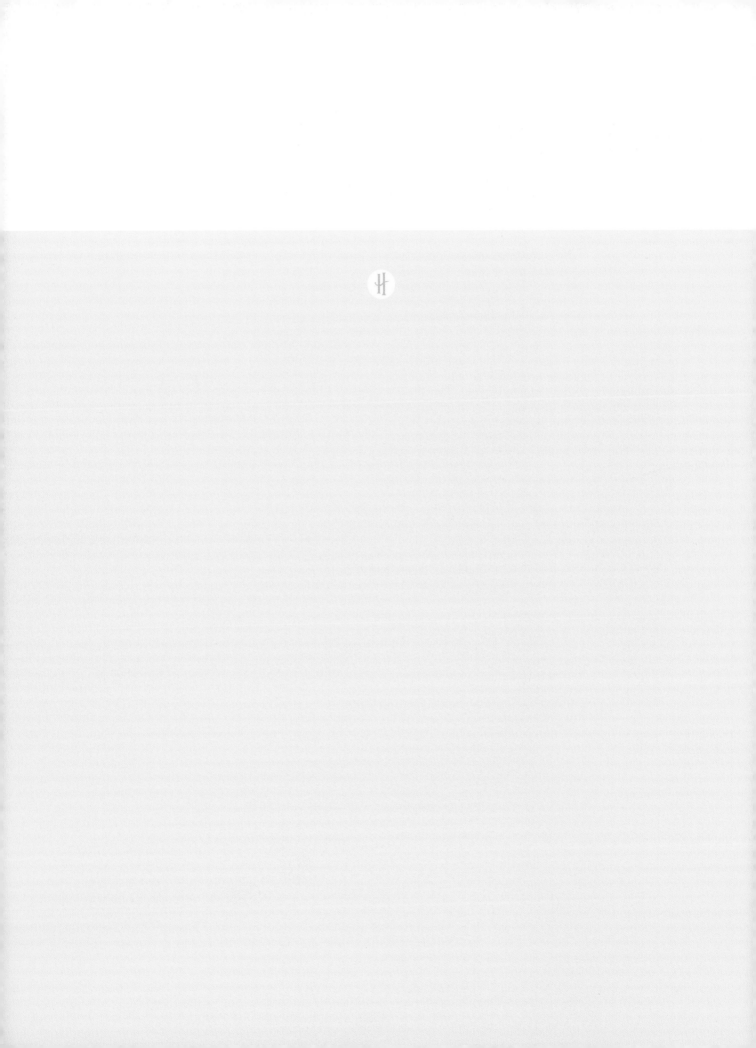

HOGWARTS CREST
III. BOTTOM RIGHT

HOGWARTS CREST
IV. BOTTOM LEFT

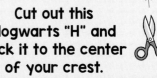

Cut out this
Hogwarts "H" and
stick it to the center
of your crest.

HATCHING NORBERT

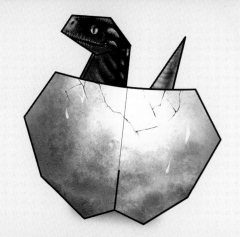

FLYING FORD ANGLIA

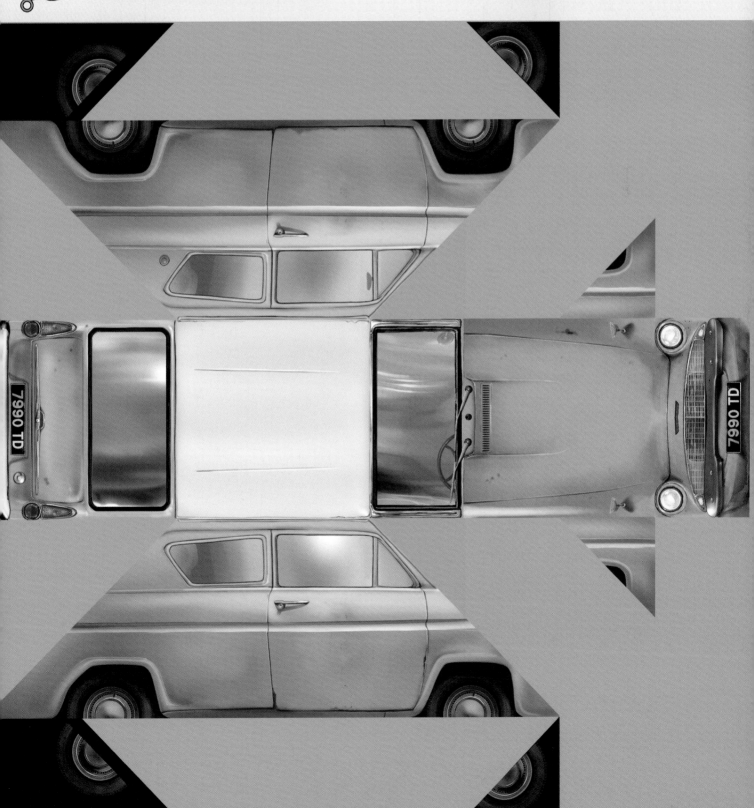

DEMENTOR

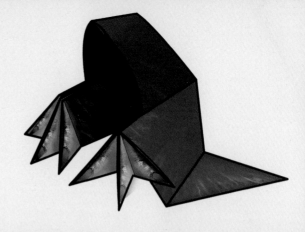

HOUSE-ELF

HAGRID'S HUT
LARGER HUT, UNIT I

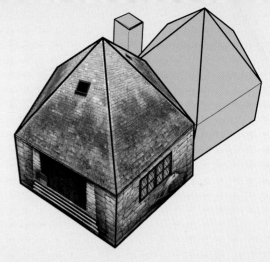

HAGRID'S HUT
LARGER HUT, UNIT II

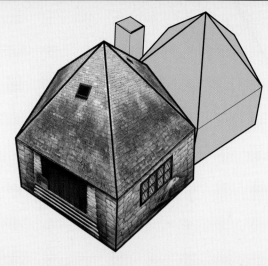

✂ →

HAGRID'S HUT
LARGER HUT, UNIT III

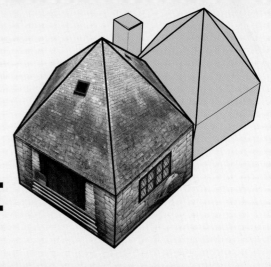

HAGRID'S HUT
LARGER HUT, UNIT IV

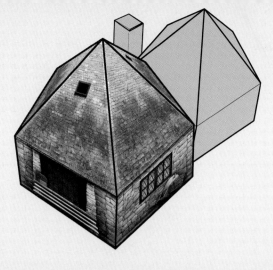

HAGRID'S HUT
LARGER HUT, UNIT V

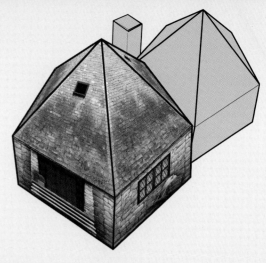

DIFFICULTY:

HAGRID'S HUT

SMALLER HUT, UNIT I

SMALLER HUT, UNIT II

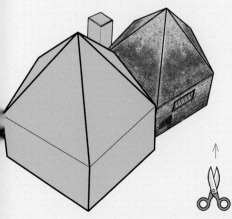

HAGRID'S HUT

SMALLER HUT, UNIT III

SMALLER HUT, UNIT IV

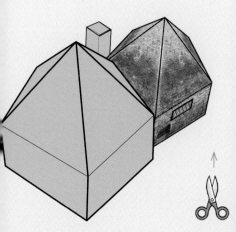

HAGRID'S HUT
SMALLER HUT, UNIT V

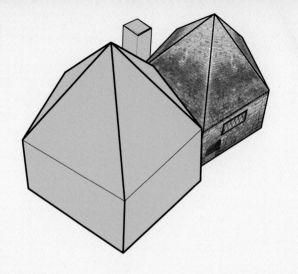

HAGRID'S HUT
CHIMNEY

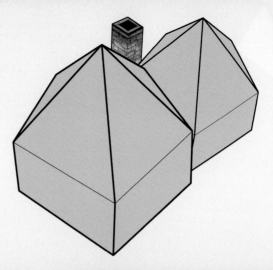

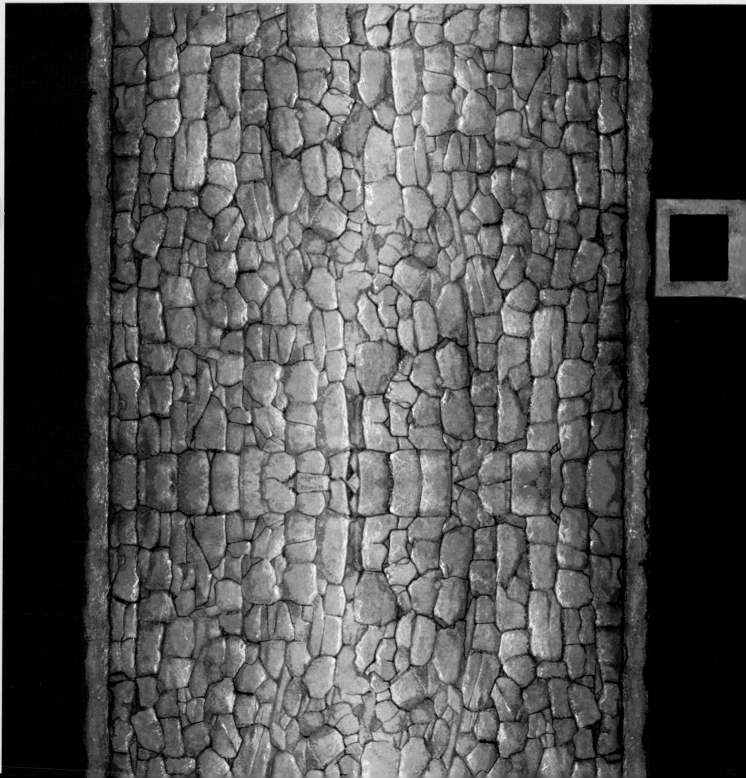